Workbook
IDEAS
&
IsSuEs
Intermediate

Editors	Carol Goodwright, Anita Gaspar
Designer	Valerie Sargent
Cover design	Gregor Arthur
Proofreader	Peter Jenkins

ISBN

Workbook:	1 899888 57 8
Student's Book:	1 899888 24 1
Double Cassette Pack:	1 899888 25 X
CD 1 (listening exercises):	1 899888 85 3
Teacher's Guide:	1 899888 31 4

Published by
Chancerel International Publishers Ltd
120 Long Acre
London WC2E 9PA
England

Printed in Italy

CONTENTS

Possibility

On page 7 we studied *might* to talk about possibility. There are other **modal verbs** we can use to talk about varying degrees of possibility. Look at these sentences.

> Eric is 16 and from Hamburg. He likes sport, supports the German football team Bayern Munich and speaks good German.

Here are some things we can say about Eric.

He <u>might</u> play football himself.	50% sure – he likes Bayern Munich
He <u>might not</u> like other teams.	
· He <u>must</u> be at school.	
He <u>can't</u> be married.	90% sure – because of his age
	– he is too young

We can use the **modal verbs** *might (not)*, *must* and *can't* to talk about what we think is true. They are all followed by the **infinitive**. Be careful! If the sentence is positive, we use *must*; but the opposite is *can't*, NOT *mustn't*! For example:

He can't be married. ✓	(he's so young, I don't believe it)
He mustn't be married. ✗	(the actual meaning here is I don't want him to be married)

1 Work in pairs. Look at the headlines from a newspaper below and discuss what each is about. There are no right or wrong answers!

Example: **Seb wins it for Britain!**

    A: Seb must be a sportsman.
    B: Yes. He might be an athlete – perhaps a runner.
    A: He might have won a medal.

16 die as snow falls again!

Rock star in court

Gladys hits 100 and still drives!

Celebration in New York!

Mother of two in tragic fall

Sam catches all his owner's fish!

2 Work in pairs. Read each sentence and decide if it is correct or not. Circle the mistakes and correct the sentences. (The mistakes might be form or use.)

Example:
    a Hurry up! You (might not) still be in the bath! *You can't still be in the bath!*
    b I'm meeting Sally today. It's been ten years since we last met, so she might recognise me!
    c Look! There's a ring on his finger! He must be married!
    d **A:** Where's Jim?
        B: He was coughing yesterday so he must be off sick.
    e One day there might be enough food to feed the world.
    f She mustn't be your mother, she looks far too young!
    g I must arrive tomorrow, or maybe on Wednesday, it all depends on the children.

Animal rights

Gerunds

On page 13 we looked at **gerunds**. These have a number of uses. For example:

a   as a noun
b   when the verb is the subject of a sentence
c   after certain verbs, e.g. *hate, like, love*
d   after prepositions e.g. *to, by, for*

> *Running is good for you.*
> *Eating meat is unacceptable to some people.*
> *I hate swimming.*
> *We are opposed to keeping birds in cages.*

1   Match the two halves of the sentences in **A** and **B**. Then decide why the gerund has been used in each. (See **a–d** above.) Example:

A
a   Experiments on animals are very important
b   You can eat more healthily
c   I'm against
d   Wearing fur
e   I hate
f   Hunting animals
g   Being vegetarian

B
i   experimenting on animals. _____
ii   is no longer fashionable. _____
iii   watching people eat meat. _____
iv   for testing new medicines. *After a preposition* _____
v   is very common these days. _____
vi   by not eating meat. _____
vii   is the only way to control numbers. _____

2   Now work in small groups and discuss the opinion in each sentence (**a–g**).
Do you agree or disagree? Why?

3   All the hidden words in the box below are from pages 10–13. Read the clues and find the words.

G	E	N	E	T	I	C	U	P	G
E	X	T	I	N	C	T	I	O	N
N	I	R	N	P	I	Y	R	A	I
E	L	A	S	I	R	X	A	C	T
S	L	P	K	U	C	R	B	H	N
M	P	C	E	F	U	O	B	E	U
O	T	M	O	U	S	E	I	R	H
A	C	T	I	V	I	S	T	N	O

a   The end of a species, when it ceases to exist
b   Someone who campaigns for a cause
c   Not only animals, but also clowns appear here!
d   All living things have these
e   Someone who hunts illegally
f   A device used for catching animals

g   A small animal often used in research
h   A kind of rodent
i   A type of engineering where genes are manipulated
j   A blood sport that many people think should be banned

The verb *get*

The verb **get** can replace several different verbs in English.

In pairs, see how many you can remember. Then, check with the examples on page 16.

We often use **get** in spoken English as a more informal alternative for certain other verbs. For example:

I'm saving up to get a car!	*get = buy*
I hate this job, serving all day and I only get £4 an hour!	*get = earn*
I got a parcel today.	*get = receive*

The **simple past** and **past participle** form of **get** is **got**.

---

1 Each sentence below contains the verb *get*. Match each meaning of *get* with a verb from the box. Then, rewrite the sentence with that new verb. Be careful! One of the verbs in the box cannot be substituted with *get*.

Example:
a   I work so hard and only get £200 a week!   *earn – I work so hard and only earn £200 a week!*
b   As I get older, I find it harder to hear people. _____
c   She never got my letter! _____
d   That film was so complicated, I didn't get it at all! _____
e   How did you get to Thailand? _____
f   I got to work half an hour late yesterday! _____
g   It gets me to see you so upset. _____

~~earn~~   become   receive   have   arrive   understand   hurt (emotionally)   travel

---

2 *Get* is also found in many common phrasal verbs. The sentences below contain *get* as a phrasal verb. Match the meaning of each with the correct definition on the right.

Example:
a   I get up at 7.30 every day.
b   My father and I have never got on.
c   What do you mean you've finished? Sit down and get on with your work!
d   The phone line was cut so we couldn't get through to them.
e   We just had enough money to get by, but it was a struggle.
f   Stop getting at me, Mum. I'm not lazy at all!
g   A car is very useful for getting about town.

i   have a good relationship
ii   attack
iii   make contact
iv   travel around
v   climb out of bed
vi   finish
vii   survive

---

3 Read the passage below and fill in the gaps with a form of *get*, either on its own or as a phrasal verb. Be careful to use the correct form of the verb!

Art used to be a difficult business. Artists didn't a **_get_** much money, often living in poor housing, with little food, struggling just to b _____. Take Van Gogh: he died mad and in poverty. Now that's all changed. Artists c _____ invitations to all the best parties, and d _____ town in big and expensive cars. On a good day they e _____ at half past two in the afternoon and f _____ to interviews three hours late, where they complain how newspapers are always g _____ them. I wish someone could h _____ to them and tell them how lucky they are. After all, modern art seems to be i _____ worse every day.

Beauty

Used to

On page 19 we saw how we can use **used to** when we talk about past habits or something that happened many times in the past, but does not happen now. For example:

> I *used to visit* my grandmother every Friday after school.
> I *didn't use to like* classical music, but now I think it's wonderful.
> *Did you use to go* to English classes? You speak very well.

How does the form of **used to** change in the **negative** and **question** forms?

1 Complete the table below with the correct form of *used to*.

VERB	AFFIRMATIVE	NEGATIVE	QUESTION
to go	*used to go*	*didn't use to go*	*did you use to go?*
to wear	_____	_____	_____
to enjoy	_____	_____	_____
to visit	_____	_____	_____

2 Below is an extract from an interview with a model, Christiana. Complete Christiana's answers using the past simple or the *used to* form of the verb in brackets. Example:

Interviewer

a When did you start your modelling career?
b Which magazines did you appear in?
c Did you travel a lot?
d What time did you use to go to sleep?

e Did you have a special name?
f Did you enjoy your job?

g What was the best thing about the job?

Christiana

I *started* _____ (start) in 1975.
I _____ (appear) in *Vogue* and *Elle* regularly.
Yes, I _____ (fly) to Paris or New York every week.
Usually at about 1am but once, on my 20th birthday,
I _____ (go) to bed at 5am!
Yes, they _____ (call) me "the legs of London"!
When I was younger, I _____ (love) it,
but it _____ (become) boring after a few years.
I _____ (love) the travel and the clothes.

3 Imagine you are retired and no longer work. Write a short description about the job you used to do, but do not say what your job was. Read your description to the class – can the other students guess what you used to be? Example:

I used to speak lots of different languages in my job and I used to travel every week. I didn't use to like flying, but I used to love visiting foreign countries and meeting different people on the plane...

Beliefs

Emphasis

On page 24 we practised using the **auxiliary verb *do*** for emphasis, particularly when the listener is doubtful and to show contrast. For example:

A	You didn't tell me your mother was coming.	B	I _did_ tell you! I told you this morning!
	I don't eat meat but I _do_ eat fish.		

Be careful not to overuse this structure! Look at these examples:

A	What time do you get up?	B	I do get up at half past six!	X
A	You never get up at half past six.	B	I _do_ get up at half past six!	✓

1 Read each sentence in **A** and write **B**'s reply using *do*, *does* or *did* to emphasise the contrast with **A**.

A

Example:
a   You don't own that car!
b   Ian doesn't speak French.
c   You didn't phone me last night.
d   You don't have any money.
e   Charlie didn't tell you.
f   Jane doesn't work with you now, right ?
g   He didn't get the letter.

B
I do own this car! _____
_____
_____
_____
_____
_____
_____

2 Look at the pairs of sentences below. Only one sentence in each pair (**a** or **b**) requires *do*, *does* or *did*. Decide which one and complete both sentences using the verb in brackets in the correct tense.

Example:
1a I don't speak French but I (speak) ___*do speak*___ German.
1b I used to live in Berlin, so I (speak) ___*speak*___ German.

2a I hate cabbage but I (like) _____ lettuce.
2b I quite like cabbage and I (like) _____ lettuce.

3a I felt better when he (apologise) _____ .
3b I was so angry with him but he (apologise) _____ .

4a "I don't think you went to work today!" "I (go) _____ to work. Ask my boss!"
4b "Where were you today?"   "I (go) _____ to work. Ask my boss!"

3 When using this structure, we stress the auxiliary verb to make the contrast or emphasis clear.

Example: *A: You don't love me.*   *B: I **do** love you!*

Work in pairs. One student reads **A** and the other **B** in exercise **1** above. When saying **B**'s sentences, be sure to put the stress in the right place!

4 Work in pairs. Write a short dialogue, between a husband and wife, who are arguing, or between a parent and naughty child. Use the *do*, *does* and *did* structure for emphasis or contrast as much as possible.
When ready, act it out to the class, paying attention to the stress. Which dialogue sounded the most natural? Were there any mistakes of form or use?

WORKBOOK

Rhetorical questions

1 On page 28 we studied rhetorical questions. When do we use them?

In the speech below a mother has just found her son smoking. Look at the questions she asks, and decide if each is a real question or a rhetorical one. Write **Q** for a real question, and **R** for a rhetorical question in the gaps below.

> I can't believe it! You've started smoking! **a** ___ Why, why do you smoke? You saw what it did to your granddad. **b** ___ Do you want to kill yourself? It's so stupid, and such a waste of money. **c** ___ I mean, do you like wasting money? I'm sure you can't afford it. **d** ___ How much do you spend on cigarettes a week?

> I just can't believe you'd be so stupid. **e** ___ Tell me, how long have you been smoking? **f** ___ When did you start? My little boy, a smoker! **g** ___ You know that cigarettes are bad for your health, don't you? **h** ___ Oh Jack, why did you have to be so stupid?

Question tags

Look at **g** above again. What do you notice about the end of the question? This is called a **question tag.** We often use them when we wish to check or confirm something. **Question tags** are made by adding an **auxiliary or modal verb** and the **subject pronoun** to the end of the sentence. If the main verb in the sentence is positive, the **auxiliary or modal verb** is negative; if it is negative, the **auxiliary or modal verb** is positive. If the sentence does not have an **auxiliary**, we form the **question tag** with *do*. For example:

> *You know that cigarettes are bad for your health, don't you?*
> POSITIVE   NEGATIVE
> *Sam hasn't been to America, has he?*
> NEGATIVE   POSITIVE

2 Complete the questions below using the correct question tag.

Example:
a You don't come from here, *do you* ?
b I gave it to you, _____ _____ ?
c Russia's the world's biggest country, _____ _____ ?
d You wouldn't lie to me, _____ _____ ?
e Sally's got flu, _____ _____ ?
f The Pottens have gone on holiday, _____ _____ ?
g You will phone me when you get there, _____ _____ ?

3 We can show if we are sure or unsure of our question by our intonation. Rising intonation shows we are unsure, while falling intonation shows we are sure.

Example: *George and Sam weren't at the party, were they?*
Meaning: I didn't see everyone at the party, so maybe I missed George and Sam.

George and Sam weren't at the party, were they?
Meaning: I saw everyone at the party, and I am sure George and Sam were not there.

Work in pairs. Take turns to ask the questions from exercise **2**, paying attention to your intonation. Your partner must listen and say if you are sure or unsure.

Discipline

Rules and obligations

On page 31 we studied different ways of talking about **rules**. Can you remember them?
For example: *supposed to*

be supposed to... is used to talk about what people or things are expected to do. For example:

> *Passengers in cars <u>are supposed to</u> wear seat belts.*
> *Cars <u>are not supposed to</u> go above 50 kph in towns.*

be allowed to... is used to talk about things which are permitted. For example:

> *Pupils at my school <u>are allowed to</u> wear jeans.*
> *We <u>are not allowed to</u> smoke in school.*

do not like... verb + ing... is used to talk about behaviour we are not happy with. For example:

> *I <u>don't like</u> her <u>being</u> out so late, but she is 21 now.*

be banned... is used to talk about something which is strictly not allowed. For example:

> *Did you know chewing gum <u>is banned</u> in Singapore? Don't take any with you!*

supposed to and **allowed to** are followed by the **base form**; **do not like** is followed by the **gerund**.

1   Complete the sentences below about the rules at a language school using *be banned*, *be allowed to*, *be supposed to* and *don't like*.

Example: **a**   Pupils under the age of 16 (not) *are not allowed* _____ to smoke.
Smoking _____ from the corridors and classrooms.
b   Alcohol _____ from all school premises.
c   The teachers _____ students arriving late,
and sometimes fine them.
d   Lessons _____ to start at 9.30 but often start a few minutes late.
e   Although the teachers _____ look smart,
students _____ wear whatever they like.
f   Language students (not) _____ to speak any language except
English, but it is very difficult when there are so many people from the same country.
g   Cheating in tests _____ ,
and anyone caught cheating is sent home.

2   What are the rules in your school or place of work? Make a list and then tell another student.
Example: *We are not allowed to chew gum.*

3   Work in pairs. At what age do you think people should be allowed to do the following?

a	get married	☐	**d**	join the army	☐	**g**	vote	☐
b	drink alchohol	☐	**e**	own a pet	☐	**h**	have a credit card	☐
c	own a mobile phone	☐	**f**	drive a car	☐	**i**	have sex	☐

WORKBOOK

Drink and drugs

Perfect tenses

Look at the text below.

> In 1997, my life was a mess. I was an alcoholic, and I could not give up. I had seen five different doctors and none of them had been able to help me. By 1999, I had lost my job and my wife and children. At the age of 26, I nearly died and spent several weeks in hospital. Then I tried the Mind Method, and it worked. What a change! Now I don't drink and I haven't smoked a cigarette for three years! Today, life is great!

Perfect tenses have the idea of *up to a moment in time*. If we are talking about a time up to the present, we use the **present perfect** (*have/has + past participle*).

I haven't smoked a cigarette for three years.   *(three years until today)*

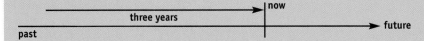

If we are talking about a period of time up to a moment in the past, we use the **past perfect** (*had + past participle*). We use the preposition **by** to refer to that time.

By 1999, I had lost my wife and children.   *(up to 1999)*

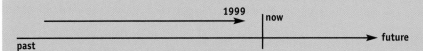

To talk about something that happened at a specific time in the past, we use the **past simple** tense.

In 1997, my life was a mess.

1   Underline the correct verb form in the sentences below.

Example: **a**   Yesterday I *had seen/<u>saw</u>* the doctor.
        b   At the age of six I *had started/started* school.
        c   My dad was in the army, and by 1996, we *had moved/moved* seven times!
        d   I can't give you a lift – I *haven't had/didn't have* a car for years!
        e   I've *been* married/*was* married for 10 years, before my wife left me last year.
        f   The letter *had arrived/arrived* by nine o'clock this morning.
        g   We *haven't seen/didn't see* them since last week.

2   Work in pairs. Read each sentence and decide if it is correct or not. If it is not correct, circle the mistake and correct the sentence. (The mistakes can be of use or form.)

Example: **a**   I've lived in this house ten years (by today.) *I've lived in this house ten years.*
        b   Mum and Dad had been married for eight years before they had their first child.
        c   I moved house in 1976 and I lived there ever since.
        d   By the end of the night, George had spent nearly all his money.
        e   By the time they are 20, most people in Britain have tried alcohol.
        f   After a wonderful three week-holiday, we finally came home.
        g   By dinner time, Lucy had already ate all her chocolates!

Family

WORKBOOK

Reported speech
We use **reported speech** to tell others what someone has said. We studied some examples on page 39.
Look at the box below to see how tenses change in **reported speech**.

DIRECT SPEECH	REPORTED SPEECH
"My name <u>is</u> Jack."	He said his name <u>was</u> Jack.
"<u>I'm going</u> to the cinema with Liz."	She said <u>she was going</u> to the cinema with Liz.

Look back at page 39 now to see how other tenses change.

1   Below are seven examples of reported speech taken from a magazine article on the problems of love and family life in the modern world. Write down what the person originally said.

Example: **a**   Jane said she wanted her freedom back.   *"I want my freedom back."*
       b   He said he'd fallen in love with another woman.   _____
       c   Maria said her parents were putting pressure on her to get married.   _____
       d   She said she didn't want to grow old alone.   _____
       e   Susan told me that she was thinking of leaving Tim.   _____
       f   Julian said he would miss his children if he left.   _____
       g   She told him it was difficult having a family and a career.   _____

2   Instead of using only *say* and *tell* as reporting verbs, you can use a range of verbs to make your writing more interesting. In this exercise, change the quote from direct speech to reported speech, using the verb in brackets.

Example: **a**   Jack: "I said some terrible things to my wife." (confess)
         Jack confessed he'd said some terrible things to his wife.
       b   Thomas: "I think arranged marriages are a good idea." (feel)
       _____
       c   Alice: "Fewer people will get married in the future." (think)
       _____
       d   Ian: "I have had an affair." (admit)
       _____
       e   Jo: "I'm getting a divorce." (announce)
       _____
       f   Sally: "I can't stop them being together." (explain)
       _____
       g   Bob: "I think that they should get married." (agree)
       _____

3   Write down your thoughts on love and family life in the 21st century. Give your sentences to another student. Put the sentences you get into reported speech and read them to the rest of the class. Example:

Pierre thought arranged marriages were a good idea.

Fashion

Comparatives

We use **comparatives** to compare two or more people or things to each other. **Comparatives** are usually formed by adding 'er' to the end of the **adjective**, but there are a number of rules. Complete the box below, using the information given.

ADJECTIVE	TYPE OF ADJECTIVE	CHANGE	COMPARATIVE
young	one syllable	add 'er'	*younger*
late	one syllable and ends in 'e'	add 'r'	
fat	one syllable and ends in vowel + consonant	double the consonant and add 'er'	
heavy	two syllables and ends in 'y'	change the 'y' to 'i' and add 'er'	
intelligent	two or more syllables	put 'more' before the adjective	
good	irregular	no rules	*better*
bad	irregular	no rules	

1 Using the information in the table above, write down the comparatives of the following adjectives.

Example: a thin   *thinner*   e wide   _____

b pretty   _____   f slim   _____

c tall   _____   g attractive _____

d bad   _____   h artistic   _____

2 On page 44 we saw how we can use verbs like *look, sound* and *feel* with adjectives. We can also use them with comparatives. Complete the sentences below with a suitable verb or comparative from the list on the right.

Example: a It's so tiring having children! I *feel* _____ 10 years older!

b I can see you've lost weight – you look _____ now.

c "How are you today?" "Not that good, doctor. In fact, I feel a lot _____ than I did yesterday."

d Oh yes, darling, I like it! You _____ so much better with short hair!

e You sound _____ on the phone.

f This bag is almost empty – that's why it feels _____ than yours.

g Listen to this tape – it _____ much clearer than the other one.

> younger
> look
> bigger
> ~~feel~~
> lighter
> sounds
> heavier
> worse
> healthier

3 Work in groups of three or four. Think of a product, for example, a type of food, a beauty product or a make of car, and write an advert comparing it to its rivals. Compare your advert with others in the class – which do you think is best?
Example:

Zazz shampoo will make your hair smell fresher than any other shampoo.
It's cheaper than Buzz…

Film and TV

WORKBOOK

Passive continuous

We use the **passive** when the **object** of a sentence is more important than the **subject** – that is, who is doing the action is not important. The **passive continuous** has the idea of *in progress* – that is, something happening at that moment in time.

The **passive continuous** is formed by the *present/past continuous of the verb to be + past participle*. For example:

The Queen is being shown around the hospital.	(**present continuous** – right now; it is not important who is showing her around)
I couldn't use the lift as it was being serviced.	(**past continuous** – at the moment I wanted to use it)

1   Change the following sentences from the active to the passive continuous. Be careful to use the correct tense: past or present.

Example:

  a   He's asking her for her name.   *She's being asked for her name.*

  b   They were painting the room yesterday.   _____

  c   Mum's washing my jeans.   _____

  d   George was moving the chairs into the lecture hall.   _____

  e   The police were questioning the man about the robbery.   _____

  f   They're teaching John at home.   _____

  g   Someone was watching Mary all the time.   _____

2   In the unit, we studied vocabulary relating to crime and violence. In the exercise below, fill in the gaps using one of the words listed.

sadistic	crimes	~~violent~~	murder	guns	copycat	terrible

Example:

  a   These days, films are more *violent*_____ than they were in the past.

  b   There was a story in the newspaper about a _____ in which a woman was stabbed to death.

  c   People who get pleasure from killing are _____ .

  d   I think it's _____ that there is so much violence in children's computer games.

  e   In America, there is a lot of violence because possession of _____ is legal.

  f   A _____ killing is one which is identical to another killing.

  g   Murder and theft are examples of _____ .

3   Complete the poem on the right using the vocabulary from the box in exercise **2**. The first letter of each word is given.

4   What is the message of the poem? Do you agree with it? Discuss with a partner.

> I see the t*errible*_____ images
> They show upon my screen,
> Of another sadistic m_____
> And I wonder what they mean.
> If we see a c_____ killing
> Out upon the street,
> Will the media apologise
> For creating this v_____ repeat?

Quantity

On page 52, we saw how we can use the expressions *too much/too many* + *noun* to say that a quantity of something is too large. We can use *(not) enough* + *noun* to say that a quantity of something is right or insufficient. For example:

You eat <u>too much</u> chocolate.	(It's bad for your health.)
There were <u>too many</u> people in the pub.	(It was crowded and unpleasant.)
I've got <u>enough</u> money for this jacket.	(The jacket is £60 and I have £65.)
There weren't <u>enough</u> cakes for everyone.	(There were five people but only four cakes.)

Many is followed by plural **countable nouns**; for example: cars, trees, burgers.
Much is followed by **uncountable nouns**; for example: cheese, news, money.
(Not) enough is followed by both types of **noun**.

1 Choose the correct expression of quantity in the following sentences.

Example: **a** £10 per ticket? I only have £5! I ~~have too much~~/*don't have enough* money!

b Well, we've got six loaves of bread, plenty of cheese and lots of fruit. There should be *too much/enough* for everyone.

c There's *too much/too many* bad news in the newspapers these days.

d We were late but we had *too much/enough* time to get to the airport.

e London's so polluted – there are *too much/too many* cars on the roads.

f Ten kids... eight tickets... Oh! I have *enough/don't have enough* tickets!

g Don't eat *too much/too many* junk food – it's very bad for you!

2 On page 50 we studied food vocabulary. Read the clues below and unjumble the words in the box on the right.

Example: **a** A medical condition where someone will not eat enough food.
A N O R E X I A

b Where animals are killed before they are eaten.

___ ___ ___ ___ ___ ___ ___ ___ ___ ___

c Basic foods. ___ ___ ___ ___ ___ ___ ___

d Slang for someone who doesn't eat meat.

e Food that is bad for you. ___ ___ ___ ___ ___ ___ ___ ___

f A farming method that keeps many animals in terrible conditions.

___ ___ ___ ___ ___ ___ ___

g A vegetarian food that is high in fat and protein.

___ ___ ___ ___ ___ ___ ___ ___ ___ ___

AA̶O̶E̶I̶X̶N̶R̶

AERHHOGUUSSLETS
SEPLATS
GIEEVG
NKUJ OFOD

YARFOCT

NPAUTE TREUTB

3 Below are some facts about British eating habits. In pairs, look at the statements and write two sentences about each. Use *too much*, *too many*, *enough* and *not enough*.

Example: **a** £1 billion is spent on advertising fast food, but only £50 million is spent on healthy eating.
Too much money is spent on advertising fast food. Not enough money is spent on advertising healthy eating.

b People eat fruit two or three times a week, but they eat meat every day.

c Fast-food restaurants are extremely busy, but health-food shops are not.

d Information on healthy eating is available, but people do not use it.

Friendship

The verb *wish*

On page 55 we looked at how to talk about things in the past we regret, *wish + past perfect*. For example:

| I ate too much last night and was sick. | I <u>wish I hadn't eaten</u> so much last night. |

If we are talking about things we would like to change about our lives now, we use
wish + past simple. For example:

| I don't have much money. | I <u>wish I had</u> more money. |

The past of **can** is **could**.
I can't speak a foreign language.   I <u>wish I could</u> speak a foreign language.

1 Every week *Saturday People* magazine runs a feature called *I wish...*, where celebrities write down their regrets and what they would like to be different. Look at the facts below from the singer Jaboo's life, and write a *wish* sentence for each.

Example: **a** I don't have much time with my family.   *I wish I had more time with my family.*

          b I argued with my grandfather on the day he died. _____

          c I split up with my first wife. _____

          d I can't write good songs. _____

          e I never learnt a musical instrument when I was young. _____

          f I left school without any qualifications. _____

          g I smoke 40 cigarettes a day. _____

          h I took drugs when I was younger. _____

2 Write out your own list of 10 wishes that you would send in to *Saturday People*.
Compare them with the wishes of other people in your class. Who has the most interesting list?

3 Match each adjective in the column on the left with its opposite adjective on the right.
Use a dictionary to help you.

Example: **a** shy   **i** proud

          b insensitive   **ii** modest

          c humble   **iii** self-confident

          d selfish   **iv** generous

          e outgoing   **v** thoughtful

          f arrogant   **vi** retiring

          g impulsive   **vii** liberal

          h conservative   **viii** cautious

4 In pairs, see how many other personality adjectives you can think of.
Which adjectives do you think describe you? What qualities do you look for in a partner or friend?

Present perfect

On page 59 we saw how we can use the **present perfect** to talk about something which started in the past and continues in the present. We use the **present simple** to refer to situations now. Compare:

> Car use in Britain <u>has grown</u> dramatically over the past 25 years. (present perfect)
> <u>There are</u> now over 20 million cars on Britain's roads. (present simple)

The **present perfect** is formed by the *auxiliary verb* have/has + past participle *of the main verb.*
Be careful – there are many irregular **past participles**!

1   In pairs, write the past participle of the following verbs.

Example: **a** need   *needed*   **e** bring   _____
              b be   _____   **f** wait   _____
              c choose _____   **g** like   _____
              d stop   _____   **h** become _____

2   Here is a recent report on rail travel. In each sentence, choose the best tense for the verb: present perfect or present simple.

> Train use in Britain *decreases/(has decreased)* significantly over the past 20 years. Today many more people *have/have had* cars, and not as many *use/have used* the train. The rail industry *has also changed/also changes*. Twenty years ago there was only one rail operator – now there *are/have been* over 20. Although numbers of passengers *go down/have gone down* since 1980, fares *rise/have risen* faster than inflation. The situation that *faces/has faced* the government today is very serious.

3   The word square below has eight words or terms from the unit on Green Issues (look at pages 58–61 to help you). See if you can find them. Can you remember what they mean?

H	U	D	N	J	R	O	R	P	F	A	M
A	P	G	R	I	E	C	V	B	A	S	P
X	O	K	U	E	S	S	L	N	C	W	Y
I	L	J	R	S	O	N	R	L	I	B	F
C	L	U	A	T	U	J	M	R	D	Y	U
F	U	E	L	B	R	H	O	V	R	Z	M
B	T	A	K	D	C	L	I	M	A	T	E
G	I	C	M	W	E	O	T	P	I	X	S
C	O	N	G	E	S	T	I	O	N	Z	B
A	N	H	T	K	P	O	C	F	W	N	A

4   Imagine it is the year 2100. Write a report on your country's traffic and public transport situation, and how it has changed over the past 100 years. Example:

> *The traffic problem has grown much worse over the last century. For example, there are now 100 million private cars on our roads...*

Second conditional

We use the **second conditional** to imagine present and future situations, and what we would do. We do not always expect the situation in the ***if clause*** to happen. For example:

If I won the lottery, I would buy a new car.
(CONDITION) (RESULT)

I would buy a new car, if I won the lottery.
(RESULT) (CONDITION)

Which tense do we use for the **condition**? How do we form the **result**?
What do you notice about the order of the **condition** and the **result** in the sentence?

1 Look at each phrase in **A** and match it with a phrase in **B**.

		A	B
Example:	**a**	If I went to London →	if I cheated in an exam
	b	I would feel guilty	I would choose a BMW
	c	I would be an actor	I'd visit the Millennium Dome
	d	I'd live in Paris	I'd take better pictures
	e	If I found a wallet on the street	I would take it to the police
	f	If I were a successful pop star	if I spoke French
	g	If I could buy a car	if I could change my job
	h	If I had a better camera	I would wear outrageous clothes

2 Look at the sentences below, and say what you would do in these situations.

Example: **a** If I won the lottery... *I'd give up work.*

b If I didn't have to work or study... ______

c If I were president of my country... ______

d If I lived on a desert island... ______

e If I could fly... ______

f If I could change one thing about my life... ______

g If I spoke every language in the world... ______

3 Work in groups of three or four and write a class questionnaire by writing five *if* statements, and three possible answers for each.

Example:

If I had more time, I'd...
a spend more time studying, of course!
b go out and party.
c read lots of books.

Compare your questionnaire with another group's and answer each other's questions.
Which group has the most interesting questions?

Language

Like

We can use *like* as a **verb**; for example: *I like chocolate*. On page 67, we saw how we can also use *like* as an **adverb**, meaning *similar to*. For example:

> He looks <u>like his father</u>.
> He speaks English <u>like a native</u>.
> It was so relaxing! It was <u>like being</u> on holiday.
> You'll never forget it – it's <u>like riding</u> a bicycle.

What types of word come after *like*? Are they **nouns**, **verbs**, **adjectives** or **gerunds**?

1 Look at the sentences below and write **V** next to them if *like* is used as a verb, and **A** if it is used as an adverb.

Example:
  a I like to have a cup of tea first thing in the morning.   *V*
  b I look a bit like my dad.   ___
  c It's so quiet in here! It's like being in a church.   ___
  d I like to go to bed early during the week.   ___
  e Ugh. I feel awful. I feel like staying in bed all day today.   ___
  f I want to have my hair very short, like my friend.   ___
  g What would you like for dinner tomorrow?   ___

2 Complete the sentences below with either a noun or a gerund.

Example:
  a The room was so small! It was like *standing* in a shoe box! (gerund)
  b You're crazy! You drive like a(n) _____ (noun)
  c It was so beautiful. It was like _____ in paradise. (gerund)
  d The coffee was horrible – it tasted like _____. (noun)
  e Her house is enormous – it's like _____ in a palace. (gerund)
  f I'm so tired. I feel like _____. (gerund)
  g Her hair was awful. It looked like a(n) _____. (noun)

3 Vocabulary. Look at the clues below and complete the crossword using the equivalent word in slang. All of the words are taken from exercise **9** on page 69.

a television
b stupid
c steal
d boy/man
e alcoholic drinks
f (see below)

_____

a *t*	*e*	f *l*	*l*	*y*	
b					
		c			
		d			
e					

When you have finished, look at the word in box **f**. This is another example of British English slang. What do you think it means? Write your answer in the space above.

New technology

Introducing examples

On page 72 we looked at how we can use certain phrases to introduce a list of examples.
We often follow phrases like *for example* or *for instance* with **nouns** or **gerunds**.

> *Boeing has produced a number of famous planes, <u>for example</u> the jumbo jet. (noun)*
> *The human race achieved many great things in the last century, <u>for instance</u> sending a man to the moon. (gerund)*

1 In this unit we saw a number of other phrases to introduce examples, and we heard some of them used by Mary De Souza. Write down as many as you can remember. If you cannot remember them all, look back at page 72.

Example: *Look at...*

2 Fill in the paragraph below with the correct phrases. Some letters have been given to help you.

Modern medicine is wonderful. T*hink* a*bout* the things they can do nowadays. T_____ _____
e_____ transplants – if your heart is diseased they can change it for a healthy one. A_____ _____
a_____ fertility? So many more couples are being helped to have children. T_____ t_____ giving
birth itself – so much safer and less painful than before. And l_____ a_____ the drugs we have now,
which have helped to destroy diseases like smallpox. A_____ e_____ _____ AZT, which helps to
control AIDS.

3 In this unit we practised words connected with the Internet. Look at the clues below and complete the puzzle. When you have all the answers, work out the anagram in the pink box (**h**) and explain what it means.

a When you are connected to the Internet.
b Something that can harm your machine, often found on the Internet.
c A shortened version of the word 'Internet'.
d To look for nothing in particular on the Internet.
e To copy something from the Internet onto your machine.
f An electronic way of sending letters.
g The machine you need to use the Internet.

Poverty

Abstract nouns

On page 75 we studied **abstract nouns**, which are used to describe ideas and qualities; for example: *goodness*. Can you remember any of the **nouns**? What do we add to **adjectives** in order to make **abstract nouns**?

1 Look at the adjectives below. In pairs, check their meanings, then write the noun form for each in the spaces below. Each dash __ represents one letter.

Example: **a** shy   *s h y n e s s*
 b timid   __ __ __ __ __ __ __ __
 c angry   __ __ __ __ __
 d weak   __ __ __ __ __ __ __ __
 e happy   __ __ __ __ __ __ __ __ __
 f confident __ __ __ __ __ __ __ __ __ __ __
 g thirsty   __ __ __ __ __ __ __
 h tired   __ __ __ __ __ __ __ __ __

2 Complete each of the following sentences with an abstract noun from the box below. Be careful! You do not need all of the nouns.

Example: **a** To prevent the problem of *lateness* we do not allow people into the theatre after the play has started.
 b Thanks to the _____ of the burglars, it was easy for the police to catch them.
 c The townspeople felt a lot of _____ that nothing was being done about homelessness.
 d My idea of _____ is a hot bath, a good book, and a box of chocolates. There's nothing better!
 e It's time for the rich countries to do their bit to fight _____.
 f Some people think animals are naturally kind, but there's a lot of _____ in nature.
 g To do a job, you must be sure you can do it – _____ in yourself is very important!

lateness	anger	carelessness	happiness	poverty	cruelty
weakness		confidence	kindness	intelligence	

3 Divide into two teams, **A** and **B**. Each team looks at the list of abstract nouns below. Using a dictionary, write down the true definition of each word on your team's list and invent two false ones for each. When both teams are ready, each team reads out a word and its three definitions. The other team must guess which definition is correct. If it guesses correctly, it wins a point.

Team A
vagrancy
clarity
scorn
hunger
coincidence

Team B
destitution
frailty
deprivation
fame
haste

Complex sentences

On page 80 we saw how we can use **what** to emphasise part of a sentence. For example:

> *What really upset me was his racist attitude.*
> *what + verb clause + verb to be + indirect object*

Here, **what** has the same meaning as *the thing that*.

1 Work in pairs. Make six sentences, using one word or phrase from each box below.

What	(made him late) I love most about Italy she was looking for in the library I really enjoyed in the film makes life difficult for some women they went on holiday for I'm hoping to buy in the sales we really need	are is (was) were	racial equality and justice for all. the beautiful photography. combining a career and a family. (a flat tyre.) the sunshine. some cheap shoes. books on American history. the delicious pasta dishes.

2 Using the key words below, write sentences expressing your own preferences.

Example:
a like my country   *What I like about my country is the weather.*
b hate about studying English _____
c annoyed me this morning   _____
d makes me laugh   _____
e look for in a boy or girlfriend _____
f wanted for my birthday   _____
g enjoy doing at the weekend   _____
h detest about computers   _____

3 Vocabulary. Look at the list below and match each word with the correct definition. All the words appear on pages 78–81.

Example:
a racism
b ethnic group
c integrate
d apartheid
e i/c3
f positive action
g National Front
h mixed marriage

i   the old political system of South Africa where people were treated differently according to race
ii to fit in with society
iii policy which favours someone because of his/her race
iv a right-wing racist political party in Britain
v   dislike for others because of the colour of his/her skin
vi people linked by a common race or culture
vii a marriage between people of different races
viii the police identification for a black person

4 Imagine you belong to an ethnic minority in your country. What problems do you have in your daily life at home, at school or at work? Make notes then write a letter to a friend explaining your problems and feelings.

Rebellion

Talking about habits

We can use **will** and **won't** + *base form* to talk about repeated actions and habits. For example:

> *Sarah <u>will waste</u> her money on things she doesn't need.*
> *She <u>won't put</u> things away after she's used them.*

We use **would** and **wouldn't** to talk about repeated actions and habits in the past. For example:

> *Uncle Tom <u>would go</u> on working, even though he was unwell.*
> *He <u>wouldn't leave</u> his old house, even though the roof leaked.*

1   June Bridges is talking about her 15-year-old son, Robert, and about her father, Albert, who died last year. Look at each statement, and write **R** if it refers to Robert and **A** if it refers to Albert. Then, write about each person's habits using *will, won't, would* or *wouldn't*. Example:

a   He spends all evening on his computer.   _R_ _He will spend all evening on his computer._

b   He never cooked a meal.   ___ _____

c   He always took the bus everywhere.   ___ _____

d   He doesn't wear anything that isn't in fashion.   ___ _____

e   He never let his children use bad language in the house.   ___ _____

f   He always spends hours in the bathroom.   ___ _____

g   He sat in that chair and smoked his pipe in the evenings.   ___ _____

2   Work in pairs. One student is **A**, the other **B**. Read your role card and prepare your part. When you are both ready, **A** starts.

Student A
Imagine you have a teenage brother or sister. Think of the habits he/she has that annoy you. When you are ready, tell Student **B** (a child psychologist) your problems. Try to use the *will/won't* structure as much as possible.

Student B
Imagine you are a child psychologist. Listen to Student **A** telling you about the problems he/she is having with his/her teenage brother or sister and try to suggest solutions.

3   Imagine you are a parent with a rebellious 17-year-old son. Read the list below of things he has done. Which do you find most and least acceptable? Number each from eight as the least acceptable to one as the most acceptable. When you have finished, compare your list with those of other students.

Has his tongue pierced! ☐

Leaves home! ☐

Starts taking drugs! ☐

Starts smoking! ☐

LEAVES SCHOOL! ☐

Comes home very late! ☐

Plays loud music! ☐

STAYS IN HIS ROOM! ☐

Sexism

The passive

On page 87 we studied the **passive** form. We use the **passive** when the **object** of a sentence is more important than the **subject**. For example:

> *Macintosh makes Apple computers.*
> This is an active sentence because the subject is important (*who* makes Apple computers).
> *Apple computers are used a lot in publishing.*
> This is a passive sentence because the object is more important than the subject (we are not interested in exactly who uses them; we are interested in the type of computer).

We make the **passive** by using the *auxiliary verb* to be + *past participle* of the main verb.

> *Our products <u>are eaten</u> all over the world.*
> *The office <u>isn't used</u> after 6pm.*
> *Where <u>are</u> they <u>made</u>?*

1 Match each sentence on the left with a sentence on the right to make a pair.

Example:
  a Ben and Zoe love Coca-Cola.   They're made in the UK.
  b Coca-Cola is the world's most popular drink.   They drink far too much of it.
  c Canada has two languages.   English and French are spoken there.
  d Sam's an expert at languages.   It's drunk everywhere.
  e Lotus makes great cars.   She speaks English and French.
  f Minis are great cars.   It makes them in the UK.

Work with a partner. Look again at each pair of sentences and decide which are active and which are passive.

2 Mick Sanders, of the pro-male group, Men Against Sexism to Men, has written an article about sexism in schools for a magazine. Read this extract from Mick's article, and fill in the gaps, using either the present simple active or the present simple passive.

... but today that's not true. Let's look at a few examples. At school, teachers **a** _make_ (make) every effort to help the girls, but boys **b** _____ (see) as troublemakers. If a girl **c** _____ (praise), that is right, but if we **d** _____ (praise) a boy, we are doing the wrong thing. Parents **e** _____ (tell) to ignore their boys and help their girls. Fine, but at school, it's boys who **f** _____ (do) much worse than girls. Boys **g** _____ (not teach) at school, they **h** _____ (ignore), and the simple reason is sexism.

What is the message that the writer is trying to get across? Do you agree or disagree? Discuss in pairs.

3 Choose someone in your class but keep his/her identity secret. Describe what that person is wearing, using the passive as much as possible. Read your description to the class and see if the other students can guess who it is. Example:

> *This person is wearing black shoes made of leather. Her blue jumper is made of wool and her earrings are made of silver...*

Direct and indirect objects

On page 92 we saw that some verbs can have two objects: **direct** and **indirect**. (Usually, the **indirect object** refers to a person.) For example:

Smith	gave	Jones	the ball.
subject + verb + indirect object + direct object			

It is important to be careful with word order and the **prepositions** you use. For example:

Smith	gave	the ball	to	Jones.
I	paid	£50	for	these football boots!
subject + verb + direct object + preposition + indirect object				

1   Work in pairs. Make six sentences with a direct and indirect object using a word or phrase from each box below. For example: *I showed the letter to a friend.*

I He Sam Cindy	(showed) gave told lent offered sent paid sold	Sarah me £5 the car (the letter) the garden a cup of tea	— (to) for	a joke the tickets £10 what happened John the book his house my wife (a friend)

2   Below are the headlines from newspaper sports stories. Put the words in each headline in the correct order. Each contains a direct and an indirect object. The first word in each sentence is provided for you.

Example: **a** swimming/sponsor/club/£10,000/gives   Sponsor *gives swimming club £10,000*

       b Leeds/for/pays/football club/player/Greek/£5 million   Leeds _____

       c drug-taking/athlete/the truth/about/Olympic/Committee/tells   Athlete_____

       d shown/player/for/foul/Juventus/red card   Juventus _____

       e team/new/hockey/to/gives/company/equipment   Company _____

       f to/athlete/prize/best/gives/club   Club _____

       g permission/to/doctor/run/athlete/refuses   Doctor _____

3   Work in pairs. Look at the word lists below and choose the sport each list refers to from the box. Use a dictionary to help you.

Example: **a** ring – referee – knock out   *boxing*

       b umpire – net – love   _____

       c try – scrum – pitch   _____

       d course – saddle – judge   _____

       e butterfly – freestyle – dive   _____

       f slalom – pole – piste   _____

       g team – foul – court   _____

rugby	soccer	TENNIS
basketball		athletics
showjumping	boxing	*skiing*
SWIMMING		*motor racing*